BEGUM AKHTAR

Love's own voice

Published in India by
Roli Books in arrangement with
Roli & Janssen BV, The Netherlands
M-75, Greater Kailash-II Market,
New Delhi 110 048, India.
Phone: ++91-11-40682000
Fax: ++91-11-29217185
Email: info@rolibooks.com
Website: rolibooks.com

ISBN: 978-81-7436-595-8

Editor: Amit Agarwal
Design: Supriya Saran
Production: Naresh Nigam

Printed and bound in India

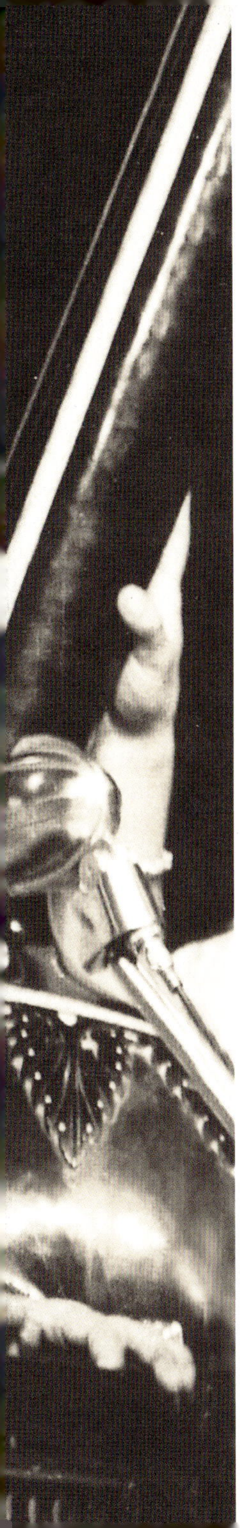

BEGUM AKHTAR

Love's own voice

S. KALIDAS

sa re ga ma
Soul of India

Lustre Press
Roli Books

To
Saleem Kidwai & Shanti Hiranand
who opened the world of
Akhtari for me

Ik lafz-e-muhabbat hai, adana sa fasaana hai,
Simte to dil-e-aashiq, faile to zamana hai.

There is a word called love, it's but a small episode,
It shrinks to fit the heart of a lover,
it expands to encompass an epoch

– Jigar Muradabaadi

THAT ENCHANTING DUO: BEGUM AKHTAR WITH FAITHFUL MUNNE KHAN ON TABLA.

The Persona

The forgotten town of Faizabad nestles next to the holy pilgrimage site of Ayodhya in Uttar Pradesh. The original capital of the erstwhile princely state of Awadh, it was once famous for its *itr* (fragrances) and its *tawaifs* (courtesans). Faizabad gave us two legendary singing women: first came Umrao Jaan, the heroine of Mirza Hadi Ruswa's early twentieth-century Urdu novel Umrao Jaan Ada[1], who still haunts the twilight zone between imagination and history. The other, closer to our own lives and very much in flesh and blood, was Begum Akhtar, who became a much-adored diva in her own tempestuous lifetime.

Witty, vibrant and engaging with the world at various levels, here was a remarkable woman who took life head-on, and by many accounts, perhaps a bit recklessly. As a *tawaif*, she was trained to charm the system and subvert narrow patriarchal practices by means of highly sophisticated and subtle seduction. At another level, she was a hapless victim, constantly tormented by the twists and turns of her own destiny. She braved on regardless, driven by a deep inner quest to pursue love in its purest form, as an end in itself – be it in music or in life. In her bewitching journey across the last century, no one – from *fakir*s to *nawab*s and *pandit*s to *pucca*-

sahibs – was immune to the charms of Akhtari Bai Faizabadi, later known to the world as Begum Akhtar.

While she was definitely captivating, Begum Akhtar was not beautiful in any conventional sense. Nevertheless, there was a twinkle in her eyes and a hauntingly melancholic quality in her voice that pierced the very souls of her admirers.

THE GULAB-BARI IN FAIZABAD IS EASILY ONE OF THE BEST KNOWN EXAMPLES OF THE ARCHITECTURAL STYLE OF THE NAWABS OF AWADH. AKHTARI'S MOTHER HAD HER HOUSE IN THIS TOWN.

Jameel Khan Ghaseete, a *fakir* devotee of the Begum's from Rampur, had once declared to me, 'There can be no *bai* (singing woman) like her ever again. She might have been a *tawaif*, but Allah be praised! What a voice! She was the Lata (Mangeshkar) of her time!' In his boyhood, Ghaseete had been

dragged by his feet (*ghaseete gaye*) across a Sufi saint's grave to cure him of delinquency. In his old age, he could be found sitting in the courtyard of a small *dargah* (Sufi shrine) singing in a soaring full-throated voice to collect alms from pious passers-by. During Muharram,[2] he would belt out the mournful *marsias* (elegies) composed by Meer Anis to the world, but would often, suddenly, break into Akhtari's *daadra*s (lilting love songs sung in Awadh and eastern UP) or *ghazal*s with an emotion so pure that it could only have been god-sent.

Nor was Begum Akhtar's fan club restricted to the likes of the plebian Ghaseete alone. A few days before she died in the October of 1974, the Begum had been in Delhi and had left some personal effects with the son of an old friend from Lucknow who had become another *mureed* (devotee). He was Saleem Kidwai, at that time a young teacher of history at the Delhi University. Saleem and his friend, Agha Shahid Ali, the poet, became more or less permanent members of her entourage in the capital in the last couple of years of her life. When she died before returning to Delhi, Saleem opened the diary that she had left behind with him to find the names of people close to her so that he could inform them of her death. The first name in the diary was that of Sheila Dhar, the wife of Indira Gandhi's principal secretary, P.N. Dhar. Begum Akhtar was immensely fond of Sheila*ji* and shared much of her private anguish, pain and many hidden secrets with her. Hailing from an old and well-known Kayastha family of Delhi, Sheila*ji* had a wonderful singing voice with a resonant timbre, and Begum Akhtar had personally arranged for her to take lessons from

SHANTI HIRANAND (EXTREME RIGHT) AND ANJALI BANNERJI ARE THE BEGUM'S TWO OLDEST DISCIPLES.

PUPIL RITA GANGULY KOTHARI (FACING PAGE) AND HER HUSBAND KESHAV KOTHARI (ABOVE) HAD A LONG-LASTING RELATIONSHIP WITH 'AMMI' AS THEY CALLED THE BEGUM.

the Kirana *gharana ustads* (masters/teachers), Niyaz Ahmed and Faiyaz Ahmed. In her inimitable style, Sheila*ji* would often regale us with endearing vignettes about the Begum. 'She had such a colourful and lively persona that there was nothing insipid about her. She was never drab, dull or predictable,' Sheila*ji* used to insist.

The longest-serving disciple of Begum Akhtar is the famous light-classical singer, Shanti Hiranand, who has written a touchingly transparent memoir of her life with the Begum. 'She was the first among *thumri* and *ghazal* singers who elevated this genre of music to the classical platform,' says Hiranand. Initiated as a pupil in 1951, Shanti was the Begum's first formal disciple and stayed close to her right until the end of the diva's colourful life. Anjali Bannerji, another early pupil, recalls her as a 'cultivated connoisseur of the good things of life'. Though Bannerji shied away from making a professional career out of music, her singing perhaps came closest to the Begum's vocalism in spirit. According to Bannerji, '*Ammi* ('mother' in Urdu) loved good perfumes, good food and drink and she hated *karela* or any bitter vegetable.' She was, by all accounts, very friendly and full of *joi de vivre*. 'She loved laughing; her pealing laughter was reminiscent of the Greek cultural icon, Melina Mercouri,' says Anjali.

Rita Ganguli Kothari is another well-known pupil of Begum Akhtar's. Of the three, Rita is visually the closest to the Begum in her flamboyant '*andaaz*' or public persona. Rita, along with her late husband, Keshav Kothari (a much loved and respected former secretary of the Sangeet Natak Akademi),

SINGER MALIKA PUKHRAJ (LEFT) AND POET KAIFI AZMI (FACING PAGE) AT THE TWENTIETH DEATH ANNIVERSARY OF BEGUM AKHTAR. RITA GANGULY (SEEN ON LEFT OF AZMI) HAD ORGANIZED THE MEMORIAL.

has also been the most active in keeping her mentor's legacy alive in the public domain. Rita had arranged a memorial concert on the twentieth anniversary of Begum Akhtar's death in 1994 for which Malika Pukhraj, the former court dancer-singer of Maharaja Hari Singh of Jammu and Kashmir, had flown down from Lahore where she lived in retirement after Partition. At the state-owned and shabby Janpath Hotel, where she was put up for the visit, Malika lit a cigarette as she

reminisced with me about her friendship with Akhtari. 'She was a very cultured woman and was never *kameeni* (mean or petty). Whenever anyone asked something from her, she always unhesitatingly obliged. For example, she used to sing this *daadra* that I liked a lot. One day I said, "Akhtari, please teach me that song", and she immediately taught it to me and wrote down the words '*Bahut din beetey saiyan ko dekhey*' ('Many days have passed since I saw my beloved...')'

Khudi ko kar buland itna ke har taqdeer se pehle,
Khuda bande se khud poochhey ki bata teri raza kya hai.

Make yourself so tall, that before every fate is decreed,
God himself asks of the man, 'Tell us what is your wish'.

– Allama Iqbal

The Making of a Diva

HAVING LOST HER TWIN IN INFANCY, AKHTARI WAS LOVED BY HER MOTHER WHO GROOMED HER FROM A VERY YOUNG AGE IN MUSIC.

Indeed, a long time has passed since Akhtari Bai Faizabadi (later to become the famous Begum Akhtar) was born in a modest home in the Gulaab-Baari area of Faizabad[3] around the year 1914. Akhtari's mother, Mushtari Bai, was a *tawaif* (courtesan), well trained in music and dance, though there are no great accounts of her prowess in these fields. She is reported to have been the mistress of a well-known civil judge of the area but had been pensioned off with her twin girls, one of whom was Akhtari. The other girl died in infancy, and that tragedy, perhaps, made the bond between Akhtari and her single mother even stronger.

By all accounts, Akhtari was a precocious child, talented and lively. In an interview given to the Rampur vocalist, Hafeez Ahmed Khan, on All India Radio in the late 1960s, she tells us how she once cut off a lock of hair from her schoolteacher, Miss Bahadur's plait one day because she found it "so beautiful". Needless to say, returning to school was not possible after that prank. Then we learn, someone set their house on fire and both mother and daughter fled to Gaya, Bihar, to take shelter at an uncle's house. Here, young Akhtari is said to have been deeply moved by the singing of a beggar-woman who used to visit their street for alms. She

RAMPUR VOCALIST USTAD HAFEEZ AHMED KHAN WAS A FRIEND OF BEGUM AKHTAR'S AND HAS RECORDED AND INTERVIEWED HER EXTENSIVELY FOR THE ALL INDIA RADIO.

would imitate the mournful wail of the *bhikaaran* (beggar-woman) with great feeling, even years later in interviews and conversations. Seeing her talent, Mushtari now decided to start her music training seriously. After some initial lessons from *sarangi-nawaz,* Imdaad Khan of Patna, Akhtari was put under the tutelage of Ustad Ata Mohammad Khan, who is said to have belonged to the Patiala school.

In 1934, an earthquake of huge magnitude devastated Bihar. A charity concert was organized in Patna to raise funds for the affected and Akhtari made her public debut as a leading singer in that event. It must be recalled that at that time, classical music was limited to princely courts and *zamindars*' (landlords) houses and public concerts of music were rare. Gandhiji's favourite Congress-woman, Sarojini Naidu, who had come to preside over the function, was very impressed by the young singer and complimented her on her musical voice.

Even before that charity concert in Patna, Akhtari had hit the stage in Calcutta, acting in plays – some old-timers remembered her playing the vamp, dressed in a black velvet Western dress and smoking a cigarette with a long black holder. She also entertained the *bhadralok* (gentry) with her music at private *mehfils* (soirées). In those early years, she looked upon the famous singer Jaddan Bai, mother of the actress Nargis, as her role model. 'Just as you look up to me these days,' she told her oldest pupil Shanti once, 'We used to look up to Jaddan Bai.' Borrowing a leaf out of Jaddan Bai's book, Akhtari went on to Bombay (now Mumbai) to act in

AKHTARIBAI ACTED IN A SPURT OF FILMS BETWEEN 1930s AND THE EARLY 1940s BUT DECIDED TO GIVE UP FILMS TO CONCENTRATE ON CLASSICAL MUSIC.

films like *Ek Din Ka Badshah* and *Nal Damayanti* in 1933. The next year she was seen in *Ameena* and *Jawaani Ka Nasha*, followed by *Naseeb Ka Chakkar* in 1935. Her dalliance with Bombay's film world continued tenuously until the early 1940s, when the producer/director, Mehboob Khan, cast her along with Kathak dancer, Sitara Devi, in *Roti*, which was released in 1942. Her last brush with cinema was in 1958 when Satyajit Ray persuaded her to play the courtesan in a charming cameo for his classic film *Jalsaghar*.

KATHAK DANCER SITARA DEVI WAS A CLOSE CONTEMPORARY WHO ALSO ACTED IN SOME FILMS WITH THE BEGUM IN THE 1930s.

However, for some reason, Akhtari dropped her film career in Bombay in 1939 and moved back home to Lucknow and set up her salon (*kotha*) in an area called Cheena Bazaar. By this time, she had made quite a name for herself both as a singer and actor, and her 78-rpm records released under the Megaphone label, were selling like hot cakes all across north India. She was now the toast of many rulers of princely states who vied with each other to have her perform in *mehfil*s and *mujra*s. This was also the time when she decided to augment her musical training and persuaded Ustad Abdul Waheed Khan of the Kirana *gharana* (school of singing) to come from Lahore to teach her. This was a curious choice, as the Ustad – nicknamed *'Behre'* (deaf) Waheed Khan, because he was said to have been hard of hearing — was a most dour, pedantic, austere and unromantic musician. He came to Lucknow for about a year and stayed as her guest. Akhtari probably felt she needed his stamp as a passport to the realms of more classically

JADDAN BAI – THE LEGENDARY ACTOR-SINGER WAS A MUCH ADMIRED INSPIRATION.

USTAD BEHRE WAHEED KHAN WAS A HIGHLY RESPECTED TEACHER AND VOCALIST OF THE KIRANA GHARANA WHO CAME TO LUCKNOW TO TEACH AKHTARI.

FACING PAGE: RECORDS SUNG BY 'MISS AKHTARI BAI', LATER KNOWN TO THE WORLD AS BEGUM AKHTAR.

inclined and 'serious' music audiences. Waheed Khan might have influenced her attitude to tonality and taught her some aspects of improvisation and elaboration of musical composition (*bandish*), but Begum Akhtar never sang the more serious *khayal* (classical form of Hindustani music, meaning 'flight of imagination'), which was the mainstay of Waheed Khan's Kirana repertoire.

This patented copyright record must not be publicly performed without licence.
MEGAPHONE
REGISTERED
TRADE MARK
HINDUSTHANI
GAZAL
J.N.G. 1152
गम को दौलत तमाम - गज़ल
غم کی دولت تمام - غزل
Miss AKHTARI BAI
(Fyzabad)
OMC. 13274
MADE IN INDIA
MEGAPHONE
SWADESHI
REG. TRADE MARK
RECORD
MADE IN
CALCUTTA
HINDUSTHANI
SONG
J.N.G. 609
केसि बांसिया बजाइ
کیسی بنسیا بجائی - ٹھمری پیلو
Miss Akhtari Bai (Fyzabad)
OMC. 5401
must not be publicly performed without licence.
MEGAPHONE
REGISTERED
TRADE MARK
HINDUSTHANI
GAZAL
J.N.G. 1152
हाय मोहब्बत हाय जवानो-गज़ल क़व्वालो
ہائے محبت ہائے جوانی - غزل قوالی
Miss AKHTARI BAI
(Fyzabad)
OMC. 13273-1
MADE IN INDIA

Patta patta boota boota haal hamara jaane hai,
Jane na jaane, gul hi na jaane, baagh tau saare
jaane hai.

Every leaf and every shrub knows of my condition,
What if the flower alone feigns ignorance,
the entire garden knows it well.

– Meer Taqui Meer

BY THE 1930s AKHTARI HAD BECOME A HIGHLY SUCCESSFUL SINGER, SOUGHT AFTER BY MANY RAJAS AND NAWABS WHO SHOWERED HER WITH RICH GIFTS.

From Bai to Begum

Akhtari's salon was on the first floor of a two-storeyed house in the Cheena Bazaar area of Lucknow. Many years later, her life-long *tabla* (percussion) player and one-time brother-in-law, Munne Khan, took Shanti Hiranand and me to see the building that Akhtari and her mother had bought for themselves. The ground floor was used as a guest apartment for visiting *ustads*, accompanists, and her extended matriarchal family. 'I used to live in a room here when I was married to her sister, Shanno,' Munne Khan told us. Akhtari and her mother, who, interestingly, was addressed by the masculine epithet of '*Bade Saab*', lived on the first floor. On most evenings, after nine o'clock, *Bade Saab* would sit chewing *paan* and smoking her *hookah* near the entrance verandah, monitoring the access to Akhtari's soirées. Only gentry of the highest social standing came visiting here.

Once, the Nawab of Rampur, H.H. Raza Ali Khan was entertained in this house. The staircase was lined with a red carpet, the banisters were hung with ropes of jasmine and new serving vessels and new furniture was bought for the occasion. Akhtari even bought a car to fetch him and drop him back. And, when the party ended, she distributed all the expensive new furniture among the nawab's entourage and presented

THIS DOUBLE STORIED HOUSE IN CHEENA BAZAAR, LUCKNOW, SAW MANY A RESPLENDENT SOIRÉE IN THE LATE 1930s AND '40s WHEN AKHTARI LIVED HERE.

the car to his son. 'In those days when you could get a *maund* (about forty kilograms) of *ghee* (clarified butter) for ten rupees she must have showered the nawab with gifts worth 50,000 rupees. You can imagine how the nawab must have reciprocated...' Munne Khan recalled.

Akhtari's liaison with Nawab Raza Ali Khan of Rampur is well known. Sheila Dhar used to recount this gem of a story: 'There was this seven-stringed necklace of Basra pearls in the Rampur collection. And from the seventh string of this necklace, hung a big diamond pendent. The nawab used to say that if there is anything more lustrous than that diamond, it is the smile of Akhtari.' In fact, so besotted was the nawab by Akhtari's charms that he is said to have even proposed *mutaa* (a temporary fixed-tenure marriage allowed in Shiite Islam) to her. However, after a couple of years Akhtari got tired of the nawab and felt terribly restricted by the court life in Rampur. One day, without telling anyone, she left the city and 'the necklace left with her...' According to Munne Khan, 'It was to escape the clutches of the nawab, that she turned her gaze towards Barrister Ishtiaq Ahmed Abbasi and married him.'

To achieve the goal of becoming a respectable homemaker was never an easy task for any *tawaif*. By the mid-1940s, most *tawaif*s aspired to that status as the social paranoia against them was getting particularly vicious. Their professional practice was being threatened by prude moralists of the religious and nationalist establishments and even the All India Radio had started demanding marriage certificates from women singers. In effecting this remarkable feat of social mobility, Akhtari chose her comrade-in-arms carefully. She befriended a highly independent and strong-willed woman, from a highly respected and aristocratic Lucknow family, by the name of Sayeeda Raza. Sayeeda was at that time working in the women's section of All India Radio where Akhtari regularly went to broadcast.

BEGUM SAYEEDA RAZA WAS A PRODUCER AT ALL INDIA RADIO LUCKNOW, WHO HELPED AKHTARI MARRY BARRISTER ABBASSI.

Five decades later, when I met her in her elegant south Delhi drawing room, Sayeeda (who later married Meer Mushtaq Ahmed, at one time the Congress mayor of Delhi), recalled her first meeting with Akhtari: 'One day in early 1944, I was sitting at my desk in AIR when Akhtari entered the room. Just seeing her gladdened my heart for we *purdah-nasheen shareef-zadis* (veil-covered and respectably born women) were not allowed to see – let alone meet – *tawaifs*. With great courtesy, Akhtari said she had to speak to me on a private matter and then politely asked if I knew Ishtiaq Ahmed Abbasi. I replied, "Of course, we know him very well – he is like family to us." Without wasting any time on preliminaries, she said, "Good, then please get me married to him." Just like that! She certainly did not believe in beating round the bush. Well, I took her request in the same direct spirit that it was stated. "I can try," I said, "I can't promise, but I shall certainly try." So I sent for Abbasi *sahib* and put it to him exactly as Akhtari had said it to me, without any preliminaries. "Ishtiaq bhai," I said, "Why don't you marry Akhtari?" As soon as I said that, he picked up my child and started playing with him, reciting a nursery rhyme. He did not answer my question, but ate the cake and snacks that I had served, and left...'

Later, Sayeeda found out that Akhtari and Abbasi *sahib* knew each other well and had been meeting secretly for a while. 'All Akhtari wanted of me was an ally – a strong supporter in Lucknow society – to further her cause. Of course, there was much gossip. People said I was naïve and did not know what I was doing, and such like...but circumstances rapidly

NAWAB RAZA ALI KHAN OF RAMPUR (LEFT) WAS MUCH BESOTTED BY AKHTARI AND EVEN OFFERED TO MARRY HER.

MR. ISHTIAQ AHMED ABBASI WITH PRIME MINISTER INDIRA GANDHI AFTER THE BEGUM'S DEMISE.

developed, and before we knew it, the wedding took place in 1945. I was present with my husband, as were Akhtari and Ishtiaq *bhai*; there was the *maulvi* (Muslim priest) sahib and one servant, Gulab. I had put my *shaadi ka dupatta* (marriage scarf) on her shoulders, and the marriage took place in Abbasi *sahib*'s office.'

BEGUM IN THE COMPANY OF FAMOUS CONTEMPORARY ARTISTS AT THE SANGEET NATAK AKADEMI.

Haan yaad mujhe tum kar lenaa aavaaz mujhe tum de lenaa,
Is raah-e-muhabbat mein koi darpaish jo mushkil aa jaaye

Yes you may remember me; yes you may give me a call,
If on the path of love you encounter any hurdle.

– Behzaad Lakhnavi

Begum Akhtar
DADRAS & THUMREES
EMI
Begum Akhtar
Ghazals
BEGUM AKHTAR
EMI
THUMRI, DADRA, POORVI

The Price of Respectability

In the white colonial-style bungalow on Havelock Road, Lucknow, which Begum Akhtar and her husband, Ishtiaq Ahmed Abbasi had bought a few years after their marriage, I met the Begum's adopted sister, Shanno *apa* (elder sister). Shanno told me that in her youth, she had been taught some Kathak by Achchhan Maharaj (Birju Maharaj's father), but had never performed. She was content managing the Begum's household and mothering children from a series of marital alliances that the Begum arranged for her. Begum Akhtar was so attached to her adopted sister that she kept Shanno with her all through her life and brought up each one of Shanno's children, as she would have her own. Shanno was a meek, loving Girl Friday to the Begum, managing the kitchen and servants. Said Shanno *apa* about Akhtari: 'Her personality was such that she loved people and they loved her in return… but above all, she was a true *Allah-wali* (godly person).'

Abbasi *sahib* was the *talukdar* of Kakori, a village not far from Lucknow, now known for its succulent Kakori *kebab*s. He was educated in England and had been called to the Bar there. He wore white bow ties and went to court in an old Chevrolet. Like most of the feudal rich of his times, Barrister Abbasi, too, was fond of music and poetry though there are no

MR AND MRS ISHTIAQ AHMED ABBASSI WITH A NIECE. LIFE AS THE BEGUM OF BARRISTER ABBASI WAS A MIXED BLESSING—SO BADLY WANTED, YET SO DIFFICULT TO BEAR.

reports of his conquests in the law courts. According to Saied Raza, who was a fervent admirer, 'He was multifaceted in his talents and could engage with people across the barriers of age, gender and class with delightful grace and ease. He was a very charming man indeed.'

Marriage brought with it the claustrophobic confines of life behind the *purdah*. Akhtari was now, finally, Begum Akhtar and music was *haraam* (forbidden). For a while she found herself playing the housewife to the hilt. She endeared herself to Abbasi *sahib*'s family; showered presents on the women and cooked elaborate meals for the men. 'She remained so devoted to, and proud of, that role right till the end,' recalled an amused Saied Raza, adding that, 'She even started signing her Urdu letters in English as Mrs. Ishtiaq Ahmed Abbasi!' Did she not miss singing in those years? 'She did miss singing,' said Sayeeda *apa*, 'But more than that she missed the whisky. And I panicked, for I had tom-tommed eulogies about her 'good conduct' and her chastity. But within the first few years of the marriage, she had started drinking and meeting people at her mother's home, and I must say that Ishtiaq *bhai* bore it all very stoically...'

The death of her mother, Mushtari a few years later sent Akhtari into a fit of deep depression, broken only by bouts of secret drinking. This was followed by the discovery of a tumour in her abdomen that caused her great pain. To bring relief from pain, a doctor prescribed Pethidine, an opioid drug, to which she got promptly and strongly addicted. Both her sister, Shanno and pupil, Shanti Hiranand who were witnesses to this time confirmed it to me in separate recorded interviews. 'But, by the grace of God, one day she gave it up herself', said Shanti, pointing to Begum Akhtar's enormous will power. Now, her husband was being pressurized by her friends and admirers to allow her to sing, at least over the radio. Many officers in the All India Radio have claimed the honour of bringing Akhtari back into the public domain as Begum Akhtar. The late Sunil Bose, himself a *thumri* singer and at that time the station director of All India Radio, Lucknow, was probably the most directly involved.

BEGUM AKHTAR FELL INTO DEPRESSION AND ILL HEALTH WITHIN A FEW YEARS OF HER MARRIAGE.

According to Sayeeda *apa*, 'Initially, Abbasi *sahib* was not convinced that this was the right thing to do, but he eventually gave her permission to sing and perform outside Lucknow, but not in that city.' I asked Saleem Kidwai if her husband understood her musical worth. 'He most certainly did,' Saleem replied, 'He understood it all the more when the world told him so and he basked in its reflected glory. In a way, he was her ultimate patron.'

When, after a silence of six troubled years, Begum Akhtar returned to professional singing via the *All India Radio*, no one could stop her soaring flight. One of the first songs she sang on her return to the studio could have been a metaphor for herself: '*Koyalia tu mat kar pukaar, karejwa laage kataar*' ('O cuckoo, don't you dare call, it pierces my heart like a knife'). She sang eloquently in Awadhi and in Bengali and had a huge following in Bengal. In the meantime, India had gained Independence and classical music was being promoted on public platforms, interestingly termed as 'music conferences'. Offers for such programmes came pouring in and soon she was performing widely across the country. As she grew in life and stature, Akhtari created small cosmopolitan islands for herself in Delhi, Bombay (Mumbai) and Calcutta (Kolkata), where she would be the unquestioned mistress of her fawning audience, away from the disapproving eyes of a staid and narrow-minded Shiite Lucknow. Fans, admirers and hangers-on followed her, and she in turn, would amuse, berate or cajole them depending up on her need, mood or fancy at the time.

AFTER SIX YEARS OF SILENCE IN PURDAH, WHEN AKHTARIBAI RETURNED TO SINGING AS BEGUM AKHTAR VIA ALL INDIA RADIO, THERE WAS NO STOPPING HER.

Ishq se tabeeyat ne zeest ka maza paaya,
Dard ki dawa paayi, dard-e-ladawa paaya

Love taught the mind the joys of life
Gave it the medicine for pain,
and gave it a pain that has no remedy

– Mirza Ghalib

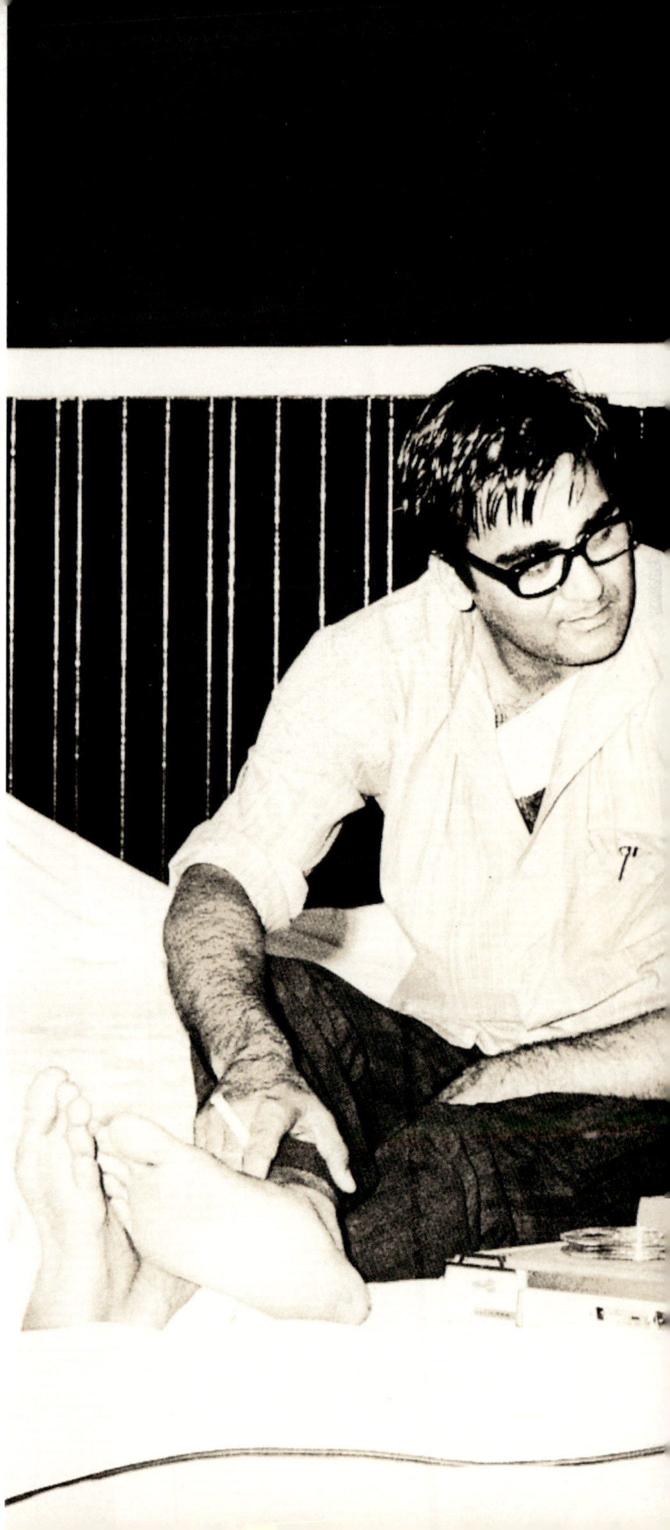

WHILE JADDAN BAI WAS A SOURCE OF INSPIRATION TO THE YOUNG AKHTARI IN THE 1930s, HER DAUGHTER NARGIS AND SON-IN-LAW SUNIL DUTT BECAME FANS OF BEGUM ALHTAR'S IN LATER LIFE. SUNIL DUTT CAN BE SEEN HERE ATTENDING A CONCERT ORGANIZED BY AJANTA ARTS IN MUMBAI.

Love as a Condition of Life

Of all the personas she donned, the one Akhtari identified with the most was that of the unrequited lover in pain. A couplet from Ghalib, whom she idolized as a poet, comes to mind: '*Ishq se tabiyat ne zeest ka maza paya, dard ki dawa payi, dard-e-ladawa paya*' ('Love taught the mind the joys of life, gave it the medicine for pain, and gave it a pain that has no remedy') Sheila Dhar believed that: 'Love was a condition of life for her.' More profoundly, Sheila*ji* elaborated: 'It was very important for her to be in love and be pained by it. If love didn't happen, she had to invent it. And if there was no pain in it, she would invent that too... She would take the smallest misunderstanding grievously to heart. The slightest injury to her 'self' would torment her like a dagger driven deep into her heart. And this imaginary dagger would remain buried in her till she had extracted every iota of painful pleasure from it.'

Sheila Dhar recounted an anecdote to illustrate this: 'In 1972, Begum Akhtar happened to be visiting the home of a leading businessman and sitarist of Mumbai when someone came in to announce that the great vocalist, Ustad Amir Khan had just died in an accident in Kolkata. As everyone in the room started to recall their associations with the deceased

ustad, Begum Akhtar kept quiet, avoiding saying anything about her relationship with Amir Khan *sahib*. Then the lady of the house made an innocuous comment, "I wonder what his poor wife must be going through." Before anyone could say anything, Begum Akhtar sharply interjected, "Which one?" and burst into a ringing peal of laughter. There was hushed silence at the uncharacteristically rude remark and soon the Begum left for her hotel.

When there was no news of her for a couple of days, the sitarist friend went to the Sea Green hotel on Marine Drive where she used to stay in Mumbai and knocked on her door. When the door opened after a few minutes, he found the Begum dishevelled, drunk and hysterically in grief. She had not changed her clothes since the visit to his house two days ago; neither had she had anything to eat. It was then that it occurred to the sitarist that in her heart the Begum had loved

USTAD AMIR KHAN OF INDORE WAS A HIGHLY REVERED ICON FOR AKHTARI AND SHE WAS DEVASTATED BY HIS SUDDEN DEATH IN AN ACCIDENT IN 1972.

Ustad Amir Khan as much as, if not more than, the *ustad*'s two legally married wives.' In the same year, film music composer, Madan Mohan, who was very close to her, also passed away.

'I don't think I will live very long now,' she told her pupil, Shanti Hiranand after Ustad Amir Khan's death. She was dead before the year ran out.

Begum Akhtar was also very gullible where rumours were concerned, and quite naïve in many ways. Minor misunderstandings often led to deep-seated grudges and that would be a constant source of trouble for her relatives, fans and students. Someone had only to hint that so-and-so had been disloyal to her and she would fly into a rage of hurt. 'That apart,' recalled Sayeeda Raza, 'Akhtari could be a great liar, too. She lied all the time, with great abandon! "Look, now you are lying again," I would tell her and she would laugh out gleefully.' She was extremely generous and affectionate, constantly showering friends and relatives with unexpected gifts and presents. 'She was a great liberal, very large-hearted and a consummate liar – all at once,' said Sayeeda, 'But when she began to sing, she would make each moment so precious that all her faults were easily forgotten and happily forgiven.' Malika Pukhraj too, endorsed this mesmerizing quality in Akhtari's music that would move her audiences beyond the expected range of emotions. 'When she sang '*deewana banana hai to deewana bana de*' ('If you wish to make me mad then so be it', a *ghazal* by Behzaad Lucknawi) people literally went mad,' said Pukhraj.

THUMRI SINGER RASOOLAN BAI WAS A FRIEND AND THE BEGUM LOVED HER MUSIC.

Ibtada-e-ishq hai rota hai kya
Aage aage dekhiye hota hai kya

It's but the beginning of love, why do you cry?
Wait and see what more is yet to come.

– Meer Taqui Meer

Elegy of an Unknown Beloved

Poor Hashmat was one such victim. The unkempt tramp was said to be a love-crazed wastrel from a noble family of Awadh. Nobody quite knew where he came from. During the day, when he was more worldly-wise, he sold lemons, onions, garlic and green chillies on the streets of old Lucknow. These were special lemons, onions, garlic and green chillies, he claimed, in his singsong call: '*Akhtari ke baag ke nimbu le lo, Akhtari ke baag ke lehsun le lo....*' ('Buy the lemons from the garden of Akhtari, buy the garlic from the garden of Akhtari.') Begum Akhtar was both amused and baffled by his antics and an embarrassed Abbasi *sahib* even got him beaten up by goons in the bazaar a couple of times. Nevertheless, Hashmat, completely consumed by his total and platonic surrender to Akhtari's bewitching persona, continued regardless.

On the night of 30 October 1974, Hashmat learnt of Akhtari's sudden demise in distant Ahmedabad through an All India Radio broadcast and went into a tizzy. He picked up a lump of charcoal and set about writing '*Hai* Akhtari!' ('Alas Akhtari!)' in bold calligraphy on the roads and walls of old Lucknow. As he wandered through the Chowk (once the red-light area of Lucknow) in a daze, his voice rang out with

Behzaad's famous lines, '*Deewana banana hai to deewana bana de, warna kahin qismat tumhe mujh sa na bana de/Ai dekhne walon mujhe hans hans ke na dekho, tumko bhi mohabbat kahin mujh sa na bana de*'. ('If it is madness that you wish for me –then make me mad, lest fate make you like me/O ye onlookers! Do not turn back and stare at me in mirth, lest love also make you mad like me').

'*Hamri atariya pe aawo sawariya, dekha-dekhi balam hui jaaye*' ('Come to my dwelling, O dark one, and we shall at least exchange glances') – it seems that these lines were sung by Akhtari in his mind's ear. As he passed row after row of hanging jasmine and rose *gajra*s, another of Akhtari's lines resonated in the dark: '*Rajaji sowtan ke lambe lambe baal, ulajh mat jaana ho raja ji*' ('O Prince, the rival has long curly tresses, don't you get entangled, my dear prince'). And much later, in the stillness of the night, as he climbed the rickety staircase of the abandoned *haveli* where he was a guard of sorts, sharing his space with a goat being fattened for the next Eid, Hashmat hummed her *daadra*, '*Bahut din beete saiyan ko dekhe...*' ('It has been a long time since I set eyes on my beloved...') and after that day no one ever heard Hashmat's voice any more.

BEGUM AKHTAR'S GRAVE IN LUCKNOW IS IN DIRE NEGLECT TODAY, COMPLETELY SURROUNDED BY RAMPANT ILLEGAL CONSTRUCTION.

Deewana banana hai to deewana bana de,
warna kahin qismat tumhe mujh sa na bana de
Ai dekhne walon mujhe hans hans ke na dekho,
tumko bhi mohabbat kahin mujh sa na bana de.

If it is madness that you wish for me –
then make me mad, lest fate make you like me
O ye onlookers!
Do not turn back and stare at me in mirth,
lest love also make you mad like me

–Behzaad Lakhnavi

Among Contemporaries and Poets

How would one place Begum Akhtar in the context of her contemporaries, Siddheshwari Devi and Rasoolan Bai? There were the obvious similarities, of course. All three came from the same socio-cultural fabric and shared the repertoire of light classical music comprising forms like the *thumri*, *kajari*, *chaiti*, *daadra* and *ghazal*. However, Siddheshwari and Rasoolan did not sing *ghazal*s much – this was the Begum's forte. Abbasi *sahib*'s contribution to her oeuvre was a highly sophisticated appreciation of Urdu poetry and she had forged close friendships with leading Urdu poets and writers. 'What distinguished her was her musical attitude. It was never over-stated,' said Sheila Dhar, adding, 'Musicians will agree with me, and Siddheshwari*ji* understood it well herself, that Begum Akhtar could conjure up a grand musical edifice within the frame of a very small canvas. Her music was rendered with a graceful simplicity. It was something that she shared most effortlessly with her audience.'

Of the two, Akhtari was good friends with Rasoolan Bai, who had stayed with her in Lucknow a couple of times. Siddheshwari Devi, the undisputed queen of Benaras, definitely better trained and far more serious in her approach to the grammar and form of classical music, was an

HISTORIAN SALEEM KIDWAI (IN BLACK) AND POET AGHA SHAHID ALI (IN WHITE) WERE TWO YOUNG FANS OF THE BEGUM AND FOLLOWED HER FROM CONCERT TO CONCERT

acknowledged rival. In fact, it could be said that Begum Akhtar and Siddheshwari Devi constituted the two polarities between which lay stretched the genre of *purab-ang gayaki* (eastern style of light classical music). In the words of Sheila Dhar: 'Rasoolan was like vintage brandy – deep and mellow. Siddheshwari was like a bird of paradise, who threw her heart and soul heavenwards with great energy and passion. Begum Akhtar's technique was much subtler. Her music was stated with an elegant restraint.'

Saleem Kidwai tells us about the Begum's interaction with the great Urdu poets of her time. 'While I did not witness her interaction with Jigar Moradabadi or Shakeel Badayuni, whose

SIDDHESHWARI DEVI WAS THE GRAND RIVAL WHO WAS BOTH RESPECTED AND DEPLORED.

*ghazal*s she sang the most, she would tell us stories about Jigar, especially, with great delight. Behzaad, we all know was like her court poet. His most famous *ghazal* '*deewana banana hai...*', it seems, was written specially for her. I did go with her to meet Firaq Gorakhpuri one day at a small hotel in Delhi's Paharganj area where he was staying. She had sung his *ghazal* the previous night at a *mehfil* and took the recording along for him. She was very close to Kaifi Azmi – there was much jest and flirtation between the two – and there were many other poets who became known just because she sang their verses.' Was she vain about the fact that she could make or break a poet? 'She was never vain. If she was proud, she never showed it. But yes, if Begum Akhtar sang a poet's verses, what more could he want?' said Saleem.

TOP: POETS SHAMIM JAIPURI (LEFT) AND KAIFI AZMI (RIGHT) WERE HER CLOSE FRIENDS.

FACING PAGE: IF RASOOLAN BAI (LEFT) WAS 'OLD BRANDY' SIDDHESHWARI DEVI (RIGHT) WAS A 'BIRD OF PARADISE' ACCORDING TO SHIELA DHAR.

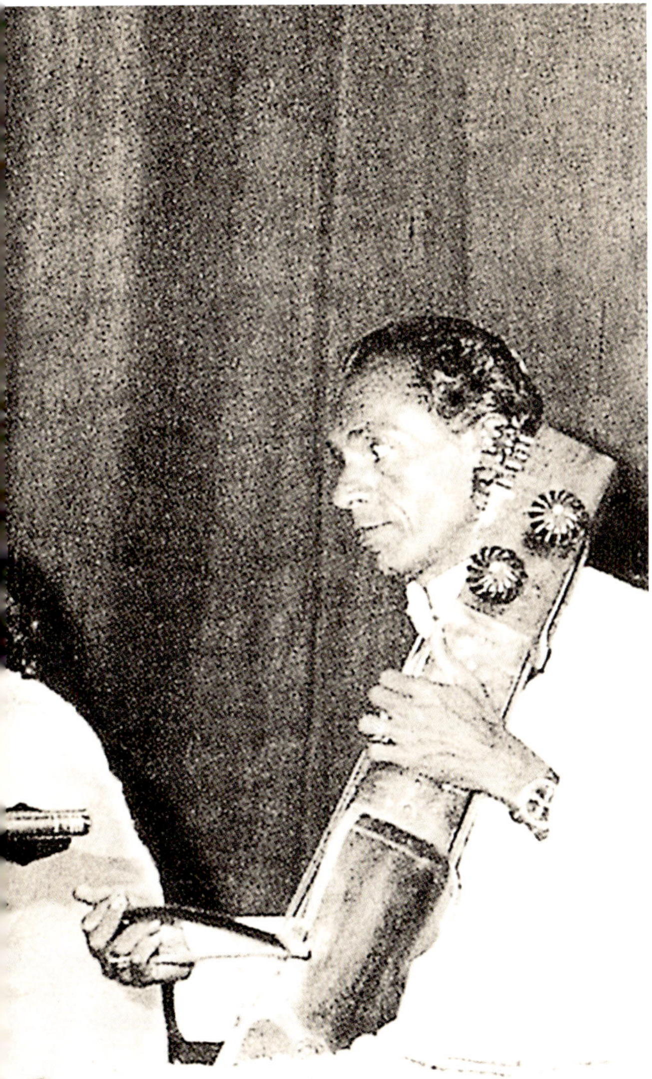

Yun to har shaam umeedon mein guzar jaati thi,
Aaj kuchh baat hai jo shaam pe rona aaya.

Ordinarily evenings would pass in anticipation,
What is it today, which makes me cry on its passing?

– Shakeel Badayuni

Epitaph

The Ghalib centenary celebrations in 1969, for which the Begum released a long-playing record of Ghalib's *ghazals*, was the last high point in her life. Begum Akhtar had now become an international icon with concerts performed in places ranging from Kabul to Karachi to Kolkata. Her career was at its peak and she was in great demand for public engagements and private *mehfils*. However, with every public high there were many private lows. She had once again started to sink into extended fits of depression and heavy drinking, often encouraged and abetted by some of her own courtiers in Delhi and Bombay. I asked Saleem Kidwai what her sorrows were. 'I think even she did not know what caused her sorrow,' said Saleem, 'At the end of her life she had achieved pretty much everything she wanted. She had her music and her admirers; there was no real want of money. But as with many great artists, she too, nursed an undefined 'need'. A need that could not be fulfilled. Perhaps, if that need were not to be there, Begum Akhtar wouldn't have been there either.'

Begum Akhtar died of a heart attack after a concert in Ahmedabad on 30 October 1974. She was buried the next day beside her mother in Lucknow's Pasand Bagh. Her husband,

Ishtiaq Ahmed, along with many admirers and disciples, bade her their last farewell. Her epitaph reads 'Begum Ishtiaq Ahmed Abbasi'.

The lasting image of Begum Akhtar that remains etched in the mind's eye is one where she is sitting cross-legged with a harmonium in front of her, one hand working its bellow with a cigarette (she smoked Capstans) between her bejewelled middle and ring fingers, the other caressing the keyboard, her eyes twinkling and her diamond nose-ring flashing as she tosses her head to spin a musical phrase: '*Aye Mohabbat tere anjaam pe rona aaya*' ('O Love, your end makes me weep') in her most popular *ghazal*. With her death ended an interpretation of love, which she alone had come to epitomize for thousands across the subcontinent from Karachi to Dhaka.

Best of the Begum's Music

Right from the mid-1930s, Begum Akhtar was a much recorded vocalist with a very wide market. Even today, one finds many more easily accessible recordings of her music in music shops and public archives than those of her contemporaries like Siddheshwari Devi or Rasoolan Bai. This was perhaps as much due to the fact of her association with films and her bewitching public persona as to her unique musical qualities like melodiousness, emotional appeal and a disarming simplicity of form. She was eclectic in her approach to *gayaki* (style of singing) and judiciously combined elements from the established individual styles of her diverse teachers and mentors from Ata Muhammad Khan of Patiala and the Calcutta-based style of the followers of Maujuddin Khan to Abdul Waheed Khan of Kirana. Besides these, of course, she was deeply and instinctively rooted in her native Awadhi (of the Lucknow-Ayodhya region) and *purabi* (eastern, from Benaras to Gaya) musical traditions, both folk and classical. She also had a wide repertoire of songs for specific occasions like coronations and marriages, religious observances like the Muharram when she sang *marsiya* and *noha* with great feeling and fervour, the Hindu spring festival of Holi and the *chaiti*

songs of March and April, and not the least, the rainy season called *sawan*.

Begum Akhtar's unquestioned metier lay in her rendering of the Urdu *ghazal*. While the *ghazal* had been sung for at least a hundred years before she arrived on the scene, Begum Akhtar's unique understanding of the Urdu language and poetry – greatly enhanced by the influence of her savant husband Ishtiaq Ahmed Abbasi – made her renderings of *ghazal*s an art form in itself. She actively sought out poets and several poets wrote exclusively for her. Many poets owed their fame more to her renderings than to any significant critical appraisal of their poems. By the end of her life, she had single-handedly managed to make *ghazal* singing an accepted form in itself, and her personal style of rendering them had become the norm; to be followed and further popularized by the likes of Mehdi Hassan, Jagjit Singh and other Mumbai *ghazal* singers.

Some Personal Favourites

Here are just a few of my personal favourites from Begum Akhtar's recorded oeuvre:

THUMRI / DAADRA/ SEASONAL SONGS

Nanandiya Kahe Maare Bol

This is an old, traditional *thumri* in *raga* Khamaj , which the Begum has rendered in a chaste *purab-ang* (eastern) style. With elaborate and leisurely explorations of both the words and the phrases of the *raga*, the Begum creates an exquisite and delicate musical edifice.

Zara Dheere Se Bolo Koi Sun Lega

A racy *daadra* in *raga* Gara, this coquettish song was written exclusively for her by the poet, Shamin Jaipuri, and is a fine example of her unabashedly seductive charm.

Chha Rahi Kali Ghata

This *kajari* (rainy season song) was one of her personal favourites too, and she recorded more than one version of

it over the decades. A gem of a song, it describes the rainy season and evokes the metaphors of love and separation with a poignancy that only she could bring to melody.

Koyaliya Tu Mat Kar Pukaar

One of her earliest recorded songs, this *daadra* (a love song set to six beats) became very popular and she recorded several versions of it, including one in the Bengali language. It is a typical *purabi daadra* in which the singer forbids the cuckoo from cooing in spring because it pierces her (already wounded) hear.

GHAZALS

Deewana Banana Hai To

This *ghazal* could be called Begum Akhtar's title song. Written by Behzaad Lucknawi and first recorded by her in her avatar of Akhtari Bai Faizabadi in the 1930s, this somewhat poetically pedestrian *ghazal* makes for some profound musical moments. As Mallika Pukhraj told me, people went into ecstasy after listening to it in her voice.

Koi Yeh Kehde Gulshan Gulshan

This is a well-known *ghazal* by the last of the great romantics of Urdu poetry, the much adored bohemian, Jigar Muradabadi. Easily one of the best from the Begum's vast repertoire, this rendering would serve well to illustrate the innate talent with which she wedded words to tunes.

Yeh Na Thi Hamari Qismat

This is a classic *ghazal* written by the tallest of Urdu poets, Mirza Assadullah Khan Ghalib. This *ghazal* has been sung by many singers and a hugely popular version sung by the actor/diva Suraiyya in the film *Mirza Ghalib* (1954, directed by Sohrab Modi, with music by Ghulam Mohammed) preceded the Begum's recorded rendering of it by over a decade. It was a difficult act to follow and the Begum more than redeemed her title of the Ghazal Queen.

Aye Mohabbat Tere Anjaam Pe Rona Aaya

This was the Begum's swan song. Towards the end of her lifetime, this Shakeel Badayuni *ghazal* set to the *raga* Bhairavi (a traditional *raga* to end concerts) was a number eagerly awaited at the conclusion of her concerts. In this poem, the poet weeps at the end of a love affair, an evening, a lifetime.

NOTES

1. Published in 1905, the novel is set in the time of the first war of Independence of 1857; *ada*, meaning grace/style/coquetry, was Umrao Jaan's *takhallus* or poetic pen name. Khushwant Singh, the renowned author, has translated the novel into English. In 1981, Muzaffar Ali made a resplendent film with Rekha playing Umrao Jaan. It was again filmed by J.P. Dutta in 2006, with Aishwarya Rai in the main role.

2. Muharram: the first month of the Islamic calendar when Shia Muslims commemorate the Battle of Karbala in ritualized mourning.

3. Faizabad, it must be recalled, used to be the capital of the province of Awadh before Nawab Asaf-Ud-Daula (AD 1775–1797) shifted the court to Lucknow.